Best Library Ever!!!

Worst President Ever

The Top-Secret Plans for Donald J. Trump's Presidential Library and Museum

Paul Orwell

Printed in the United States of America

First Printing: April 2020

Published by Oceania Press

ISBN-13 978-1-7338073-3-3

ISBN-10 1-7338073-3-3

TABLE OF CONTENTS

Preface

COVID-19 IS NO LAUGHING MATTER. OUR NATION faces an uncertain and scary future. But life still has to be lived, and laughter – like love and now loss – will continue. I am inspired by the steadiness and serious-ness of governors like Andrew Cuomo (D-New York), Mike DeWine (R-Ohio), Larry Hogan (R-Maryland), and others. I am shell-shocked that when faced with the opportunity and moral obligation to bind this nation together, our angry president continues to smart and tear it apart. In November, we need the orange clown from Queens to exit stage left and focus instead on building his presidential library – the BEST LIBRARY EVER!!! – which is the subject of this book.

* * *

THE FIRST TIME I WENT TO A PUBLIC LIBRARY, I thought, "Wow, that's a lot of books!" In 2026, when I walk into the Donald J. Trump Presidential Library, I'll think, "Wow, no books at all!"

Yes, Trump's presidential library will be different. It will be a big freaking freakshow of wrestling villains and superheroes, a circus where Donald the ringleader-king saves the world and bows to wild applause. His library will, tweet-by-tweet, relentlessly revise, pitch, and demolish what most people would call facts (or history) and bend the truth past its breaking point to glorify himself. Books? Is that a joke? – Donald can barely even read!

I've been to most of the presidential libraries in America. They are all different but this one will be really, *really* different. After visiting it, part of you will know that this library is a joke, but you'll still feel queasy. All that screaming and fist-waving ... and was that really a *tooth* you saw rolling across the floor? Must the world, with people dying by the thousands be divided into winners and losers? Surely facts shouldn't be fungible? And isn't Don still trying a little too hard to impress us?

The Orange Menace will not like my book but he's unlikely to ever read it. So, I ask you, Dear Reader, to remember that satire (and criticism) aimed at political issues, are the most-protected form of free speech under the First Amendment.

But back again to those library books of my youth. Through them, I learned that truth really *does* matter. Today when I take a favorite volume off a library shelf, the page I read forty years ago is still the same page –

its words didn't change; the truth hasn't changed. Remember that as you drive up Ivanka Avenue past the Statue of Trumpety and toward the Best Library Ever (!!!) – you are in for a gravity-defying and truth-denying ride.

Introduction
Oh, Yes. Every
President Gets One!

WRAP YOUR HEAD AROUND THIS: WHEN TRUMP'S done he's going to get his own presidential library if he wants one – which he will.

The good news is that private donations will pay for the library's construction. The bad news is that once it's built, the federal government will take over its maintenance and operations for the everlasting public good and at the expense of the American people.

What will this library – the library of a man who famously avoids reading – even look like? Leaked, top-secret plans reveal all the details:

- Chapter 1 breaks down where Trump's library might be located, how big it will be, its style, and how it brings to life the future once imagined by George Orwell, where "The past was erased, the erasure was forgotten, the lie became the truth."[1]
- Chapter 2 takes a quick look at past presidents' libraries to see how they might influence Trump's decisions. Or not.

- Chapter 3 reveals the leaked plans for Don's library and takes an exciting tour through the museum's key rooms and exhibits. **Read just one chapter? Read this one.**
- Chapter 4 briefly summarizes the laws and legislation governing presidential museums and their funding.
- Chapter 5 explores how Trump will exploit these laws and pocket tremendous profit.
- Finally, Chapter 6 imagines the aftermath of Don's electoral defeat in 2020 and how that will affect his and his library's legacy.

WHETHER THE DONALD J. TRUMP PRESIDENTIAL Library and Museum ends up being an architectural wonder or a monstrosity will be a matter of taste, but in Trump's own opinion, it will be "BEST LIE-BERRY ever!"

Chapter 1
Decisions, Decisions!

DONALD "NOBODY CAN BUILD LIKE ME" TRUMP will face many decisions when he sits down to think about his future presidential library and museum.[1]

- Where will it be? Which state? Which city and why?
- How big will it be? Size matters. Size really matters.
- Will it be more of a library, more of a museum, or more of an "experience"? (I think we know the answer to this one.)
- Style. Will it be a Parthenon-style building or a skyscraper, and what will it look like inside?
- How much money will be needed from his donors (or his own pocket) to build what he desires? His donor pool will be much smaller if Don is in jail or living in Moscow than it would be if he has a primetime show on Fox News or is living high on the hog in Florida.
- How can he turn this into a money-making venture?

WHERE O WHERE WILL IT BE?

It's a maxim of real estate that "location, location, location" are the three factors that determine the desirability of a property – something Don is keenly aware of.

A presidential library's location is the personal decision of the ex-president, but donors, financiers, zoning laws, budget, sunshine hours, and proximity to golf courses can all factor into the mix. Often, presidential libraries are located in or near a president's hometown. So, New York City would likely be a top contender on Don's list. Born in Queens, he spent most of his adult life in Manhattan, but was and is continuously snubbed by the moneyed elites living there.

If he proposed Manhattan for his library, mobs would march against it, the mayor would say no to it, the legislature would block it, residents would shun it, and it would be expensive for the police and army to protect it from protesters and defacement. And he can't afford it.

New York City might be Don's hometown, but he's no hometown favorite. In the 2016 election, Clinton beat Trump 9:1 in Manhattan – 9:1 in his *hometown*!! That's how unpopular he is with his fellow Manhattanites.

No, Don will look elsewhere for a location because

he doesn't want to be hissed at on the streets of his hometown for the rest of his life.

So, where to go?

What about Washington, D.C.? Perhaps his failing (nearly half-empty) hotel in the Old Post Office, ranked the third worst in the world by Luxury Travel Intelligence, would see greater success if converted into his library.[2] But Trump can't do that because he doesn't own the property. He leases it from the federal government and it's illegal to use federal land for a presidential museum. Plus, he lost the presidential vote in the District of Columbia by 20:1, so it too will likely be stricken from his list.

Well, there's plenty of space among his supporters out in the Midwest and Mountain States. Don could put it in the suitably named Crook County, Wyoming, where – wow – he got 87% of the vote versus Clinton's 7%. But Crook County is in the middle of nowhere, and the name Crook County probably doesn't appeal.

Don's library would be welcome in West Virginia, too, where 68% of the vote went to Trump over Clinton's 26%. He'd find tons of cheap coal there to power the lights, but is this really the kind of place where Don wants to hang out post-presidency? He's more of a sunshine and tan (fake tan) kind of guy.

Can't be Atlantic City. Don's already been there, done that, and left the scars to prove it. No, I think the 15th presidential library will almost certainly go to ...

sunny Florida. Agent Orange changed his official residency to the Sunshine State in 2019, in part because he needs Florida to win re-election in 2020, but also because the taxes are lower there.

As his new home state, Florida offers up several good locations for a library. First, he could use Mar-a-Lago itself, or the two houses he owns next door to it, or he could combine those residences with Mar-a-Lago.

Another possibility would be converting part of his failing National Doral golf complex (where net operating income has dropped by 69% since 2017).[3] This is the same "perfect" resort where Trump planned to host the 2020 G-7 summit, or at least he was until bipartisan blowback from Congress led him to walk back the award. It has more space than Mar-a-Lago and includes a 25,000-square-foot ballroom that could house part of his museum. With Doral's revenue falling, this might be a good way to turn a loser into a winner – plus, if he needs more space to make the library even bigger, he could dig up the greens of the resort's so-called Red Tiger or Blue Monster golf courses (I'm not making these names up). Then again, he could just knock a few walls down and reuse the deserted conference center there.

Briny Breezes has been floated as another possible site. Though it sounds like the smell from a waste disposal unit, Briny Breezes is a 43-acre trailer park, one of only two trailer parks in Florida that are incorporated towns. It lies 12 miles south of Mar-a-Lago on a barrier island between the Atlantic and the Intracoastal Waterway – a prime location that Don has shown an interest in over the years.[4] The problem is, the asking price is a cool one billion dollars. Don doesn't have that kind of moolah and his donors won't stump it up for him. Plus, whether Don denies that global warming exists or not, it is vulnerable to rising sea levels – and even more briny breezes.

If Trump selects one of these Florida locations for his library, he'll likely get his name emblazoned on another public edifice, too – once West Palm Beach Airport is renamed the Donald J. Trump International Airport. Imagine flying into DJT! You'll board a shiny golden bus to be shuttled five miles to the library, which will drive down MAGA Boulevard (formerly Australian Avenue), along Witch Hunt Way (formerly Southern Boulevard), take the bridge over Lake Net Worth (formerly Lake Worth), then turn on Ivanka Avenue to the library's main entrance.

Factors such as cash flow may come in to play in the library's site selection. If Trump is hard-up or broke (which he would be if his loans were called in, forcing him to fire-sale his real estate assets), donating Mar-a-Lago to the U.S. government might not appeal at first. However, his presidential library committee could buy it from him at an inflated price, THEN donate it to the U.S. government.

Billionaires to the rescue! That's definitely a possibility.

SIZE MATTERS. IT REALLY DOES.

Size means a lot to Don. To him, big is truly beautiful. He'll naturally want his presidential library to be the largest and most expensive ever, but it will be hard to top the massive footprint of Ronald Reagan's facility, which currently ranks first in terms of physical size. With a 2005 expansion, Reagan's library outbuilt and took the record from The Clinton Presidential Library and Museum. It constructed a 90,000-square-foot building to house a single exhibit, the Boeing 707 that served as Air Force One to seven presidents, and that structure alone is bigger than Mar-a-Lago.

If Trump builds his library in Florida at one of the likely locations, it won't measure up. And taking the lead position from Reagan would be absolutely impossible in Manhattan. The man to whom size really matters may find his library relegated to the boonies in order to be the biggest. Otherwise, he'll certainly spew other superlatives about his edifice, with its beautiful balconies and proud palms, desirably located in the middle of the east coast of Florida, or that it's the 22nd-largest mansion in the whole of the U.S.[5]

BOOKS? WHAT BOOKS?

Presidential libraries and museums are typically co-located, but people rarely go there to look through a bunch of old archives. Besides, Don doesn't read or write much, so there won't be much in the way of books, just a few shelves of remaindered *The Art of the Deal* and a showcase of Sharpie weather doodles.

Instead, he'll focus on the museum aspect, but not in the traditional sense. His museum will continue to blur the line between fact and fiction that defined his presidency, perhaps offering an experience celebrating all things Trump that emphasizes aspiration and story-telling over truth.

Of course, cold hard cash will be front, right, and center. Visitors will be monetized much more aggressively than at any other presidential library. You won't find an old lady shaking a tin to collect money for the troops – nope! Instead there will be wide-eyed, sun-kissed cheerleaders giving hugs for a buck, and $50 buys the opportunity to toss Clinton dolls to the alligators. The house always wins, and I guarantee you *will* leave with substantially less money than you went in with.

STYLE MAKETH THE MAN

While many consider Trump a destroyer – of freedom, morals, tradition, and civil discourse – Trump likes to think of himself as a builder, constructing towering skyscrapers all over the world and projecting his wealth for all to see. His presidential library will provide proof in perpetuity that backs up his core belief.

I am the BEST builder, just look at what I've built. Hillary can't build.

—@realDonaldTrump, May 13, 2015[6]

BUT IT'S WHAT'S INSIDE THAT COUNTS, AND A LOOK within his properties reveals much about the man. Trump's style might be called "lacking in taste" in polite parlance, but author Peter York suggests that his aesthetic is quite recognizable as "dictator chic": it's the fashion favored by infamous autocrats of the last century, a style that dictates grandiose scale and "a positive blizzard of [fake] gold."[7]

Trump's library will emulate the opulent architecture of ancient Roman baths and Greek temples. For its interior spaces, think Versailles, or Elvis's Graceland. And the Trumpian décor inside will be saturated with gold, the preferred color of dictators and wheeler-dealers like Trump:

The Golden Rule of Negotiating: He who has the gold makes the rules.

—@realDonaldTrump, July 30, 2013[8]

Golden carpet, gold drapes, gold fountains and Roman columns, even gilded goldfish dispensing the toilet paper. Gilding is a perfect metaphor for Trump. The process applies a tiny amount of real gold – one tenth of one millionth of a meter – to a surface,[9] giving it the sheen of luxury, but it remains the same base material underneath.

Just like Don. He might look presidential now, but underneath he's still the same thick thug as ever.

MONEY MONEY MONEY: IT'S A RICH MAN'S WORLD

The New Testament tells the story of the conversion of Saul. On the road to Damascus, the hate-filled money-lender saw the light and was converted to spread the word of Jesus. When Trump leaves 1600 Pennsylvania Avenue, he will not have this kind of conversion. No, he will have a "reversion" back to where was before, where his mind always goes – to money – and his actions will fall back to the familiar: to television, boasting, gloating, lying, and trying to keep his hotels and golf courses afloat.

* * *

GLOBAL WARMING WARNING

Trump Doral lies just three feet above sea level, so as the poles melt you'll need a canoe to reach his library if he builds it there. Mar-a-Lago's situated a bit higher, but you'll need one there soon enough! Or an airboat.

Chapter 2
Them That Came
Before Him — 14
Presidential Libraries

Go to the Guided Tour in Chapter 3 if you want to skip this short history chapter.

DONALD TRUMP'S WILL BE THE 15TH OFFICIAL presidential library and museum. How will it compare to the earlier ones? Screw that – Don won't care! Never one for tradition or sentiment, he will focus on what his library means for *his* pocket and *his* image. (But he'll still want his library to be bigger and better than any that came before.)

Visiting a presidential museum gives you a feeling for the weight of the office of President of the United States and a sense of the rhythm of the times in which they lived and served. For example, the Second World War plays a crucial part in FDR's museum in Hyde Park, New York. It's also important in Dwight Eisenhower's museum. Though he did not become president until 1953, eight years after the war ended, Eisenhower was nonetheless deeply involved in directing military operations. The five-star general was appointed Supreme Allied

Commander in Europe and charged with executing Operation Overlord – D-Day and the Western Allied invasion of Germany. Eisenhower's museum also incorporates his modest boyhood home and conveys the good midwestern morals of the man from Abilene, Kansas.

By comparison, the Trump years have been a bit of yawn in terms of history until the coronavirus came along, when yawning might prove fatal. He did manage to give away a few billion dollars in tax cuts to his pals and bromance Kim Jong-un and Vladimir Putin, but he never consummated those relationships. No, nothing much happened on his watch until coronavirus COVID-19 came along (dismissed as another Democratic "hoax"), but the master of chaos is always stirring up shit, attracting a perpetual swarm of flies buzzing around. We're all exhausted by it, annoyed by the pests, the pestilence, and the putrid smell.

Trump's museum might go the way of Herbert Hoover's instead and cover his pre-term life in great detail. Hoover's success and travels as a businessman and mining engineer, and his term as Secretary of Commerce (1921–1928) are extensively recounted by his museum. Or Trump's museum might begin his story with his campaign, similar to the library of George W. Bush, a.k.a. Bush Junior, Bush 43, or Shrub. His museum largely picks up when Bush ran for office in 2000, despite his earlier political experience as Governor of

Texas and the elder Bush's terms as vice president and president.

Important men and women – vice presidents, key advisers, wives, and children – feature prominently in all other presidential museums but most presidents don't have as many as Don – not as many cabinet secretaries, chiefs of staff, or wives. Many came and many went. Many went to jail. Many got the boot or were divorced. How would that many wax figures even fit into one room ... and wait, was that guy Homeland Security Secretary 4 or Chief of Staff 2?

Other presidential libraries honor dignitaries like Martin Luther King Jr. and Bobby Kennedy, or even mention opponents such as Newt Gingrich's appearance in Bill Clinton's. There'll be none at Don's. He won't share the stage or the spotlight with anyone.

TAKE A TRIP ACROSS AMERICA – GO VISIT!

You really should! Visiting presidential libraries and traveling to the different states where they're located will teach you a lot about the good people of this country. Head into the Simi Valley mountains to Reagan's hilltop museum, stare out over Boston harbor from JFK's. Go to Hoover's museum in West Branch ... where's that? In case you don't know, that's in Iowa. Go to Abilene, Kansas (Eisenhower), or Yorba Linda, California (Nixon), or Austin, Texas (LBJ). You're out of luck in Mountain Time Zone or Florida (at least for now).

Presidential libraries and museums are set in beautiful, spacious, park-like grounds and a trip to each is time very well spent. The kids can run around, grandpa can get a cup of coffee, and you can look at the exhibits and reminisce. The artifacts, photographs, newspaper headlines, and TV broadcasts within the museums bring the past to life. You will find them nostalgic (if you're old enough) and historic (if you're not). An annual membership to an individual museum is not only inexpensive, it's reciprocal.

It's hard not to be impressed by these men's commitment to politics and public service. For all the chatter about ex-presidents profiting from the office, money was never the reason they entered politics – they did so because they were driven to, usually for life. Never for the salary, which is currently set at $400,000 annually (it was $200,000 in the 1980s and lower still – just $100,000 – in the 1960s).[1]

Presidential libraries and museums have gotten more partisan over time but are still enjoyable by all. They're a little biased but not too self-congratulatory, boastful, or overtly offensive to members of the opposite party. Even though events from history can still divide opinion – take the Gulf War, for example – the museums try to remain *somewhat* evenhanded, to explain and justify but not to judge.

A Democrat would not feel unwelcome at Ronald Reagan's magnificent mountaintop library. A Republican would be received hospitably at Bill Clinton's museum in Little Rock. And I am sure Barack Obama's museum, when it opens in Chicago, will take care to be balanced so that citizens of both parties can gain an understanding of the challenges and achievements he faced — even though they divided Congress at the time.

Take a visit — and take in the diversity of America and all Americans.

Chapter 3
The Guided Tour

Trump's library and museum won't look like those of previous presidents and Don won't care. He's never been concerned by protocol or precedent, a trait that makes his supporters even more loyal. And though libraries are repositories where people typically seek truth and knowledge, the exhibits in his museum won't have anything to do with truth: a better name for his might be a lie-brary. Its objectives are to position him as a prophet, praise his farcical legacy, pitch his business and investment acumen, and provide plenty of opportunities for visitors to open their pocketbooks.

To Democrats, it'll be a heap of hucksterism. To his supporters, it will be totally and utterly fabulous, like a 24/7 rally. It will be unmistakably pure Trump.

TOP SECRET PLANS REVEALED!

We received an unmarked envelope containing the plans from a John Barron within Don's administration. A later search found no record of anyone by that name on the White House staff, ever. An examination of the extremely small fingerprints on the plans could not positively confirm John's identity.

UP IVANKA AVENUE

The golden Trump buses (petroleum-fueled, of course) will chug up Ivanka Avenue from Witch Hunt Way toward the main entrance. Don's voice will announce false facts about his museum over the unlicensed background track of The Rolling Stones hit "You Can't Always Get What You Want."

The bus will drive past the Statue of Trumpety (see book's front cover) which shows Demander-in-Chief Don at his defiant and angry best, raging at the wind, holding a tablet of lies. Don's plans specify that its color should match Fluorescent (or Florida) Orange (Pantone 021C) – a shade he deems "Trump in good health" but critics call "orange clown," "bullshit," or "vomit" orange. Some find it kind of spooky-looking, the way the white eye sockets poke out of his crispy, toaster-oven skin.

Then the bus rumbles through an outdoor installation with sculptures of iron exclamation marks in different sizes, leaching rust into the water table. To some, it looks like chaos, while others find it "perfect," and the bus smogs on to its destination: Don's library.

MAIN ENTRANCE

Facial recognition software will efficiently route the rich and poor through separate turnstiles and update Republican polling databases. Armed burly men wearing MAGA hats will push the weakest and poorest to the back of the holding pens. Facemasks are not allowed; weapons will be. Anyone with a pre-existing condition will be denied entry without proof of insurance. Supporters get a meaty Patriot's Discount by showing their NRA membership cards, while priority access is granted to VIPs and anyone who has pre-paid $1,000 for a Trump Steak Special at the museum's café (toured later in this chapter). Visitors can cut the line by paying $25,000 on the spot and earn a dinner date/plate with Don and a *free* thumb-ups photo!

A pair of enormous marble lions stand guard outside the majestic main entrance. The statues are modeled after actual trophies borrowed from the extensive collection of Donald Trump, Jr. and are six inches taller than the lions at the New York Public Library. The structure's façade bears the iconic Trump name, below which appears the inscription *In My Great and Unmatched Wisdom*.

THE GRAND HALL (OF SMOKE AND MIRRORS)

Once inside, the myth of prosperity will be spun ... and spun and spun and spun. Trump's spotty business history will be bleached, washed, and retold as a rag-to-riches, "everything he touches turns to gold" fable, with no mention of his bankruptcies and bullying, his lawsuits and losses.

A piped-in voice – perhaps Ivanka's – fills the hall and his tale unfolds. As a young man, Don was handed a dollar by his father (just a small loan!), and by his own labors, built a fortune of trillions and gazillions of dollars. That's the story his supporters want to hear because they want to believe it could be true *for themselves* – "maybe I can get lucky and live this way too!"

An enormous map stretches from floor to ceiling along one wall, showing all the Trump properties around the world – even those that have already removed his name or been rebranded. A digital display projects the total number of square feet of all the buildings that have ever been under Don's control – millions and billions of square feet – and visitors gasp with delight each time the number jumps higher.

To Don, appearances matter and money is the best measure of success. His library will make him appear to be the richest and most successful person history has ever known.

TEMPLE OF TWEETS

Immerse yourself in pure, unfiltered Trump in this tribute to his crowning achievement as the nation's Tweeter in Chief. Learn how he used this nascent medium to revolutionize presidential communication, amass over 70 million followers, and eliminate the need for traditional media by personally broadcasting his most consequential decisions in 280 characters or less.

Gigantic videos screens – much bigger (of course) than the ones in Times Square – deliver a running feed of Trump's most famous tweets, to the delight of his fans:

Sorry losers and haters, but my I.Q. is one of the highest -and you all know it! Please don't feel so stupid or insecure, it's not your fault.

—@realDonaldTrump, May 8, 2013[1]

North Korean Leader Kim Jong Un just stated that the "Nuclear Button is on his desk at all times." Will someone from his depleted and food starved regime please inform him that I too have a Nuclear Button, but it is a much bigger & more powerful one than his, and my Button works!

—@realDonaldTrump, January 2, 2018[2]

Crazy Joe Biden is trying to act like a tough guy. Actually, he is weak, both mentally and physically, and yet he threatens me, for the second time, with physical assault. He doesn't know me, but he would go down fast and hard, crying all the way. Don't threaten people Joe!

—@realDonaldTrump, March 22, 2018[3]

Despite the constant negative press covfefe

—@realDonaldTrump, May 21, 2017 (deleted)[4]

Every time I speak of the haters and losers I do so with great love and affection. They cannot help the fact that they were born fucked up!

—@realDonaldTrump, September 28, 2014[5]

For an enhanced experience, the exhibit's audio tour presents a curation of Trump's "best words" intoned by the voice of God, or someone who sounds like Morgan Freeman. Smartphone users can access the tour via the official museum app (which will track them as they walk around the exhibits), while headsets will be available from rental kiosks.

The exhibit's interactive nature gets visitors involved by promoting active citizenship. Huge "Like" buttons placed throughout the interactive exhibit allow visitors to vote for their favorite tweets as many times as they want, then watch as the numbers keep going up! Poster-sized prints of the winningest tweets of all time are available for purchase in the gift store.

The museum recognizes that these tweets represent a significant portion of the president's historical record, and as such, there will be no corrections made to punctuation or spelling. Management reserves the right to eject elites expressing editorial criticism or who refer to the exhibition as "The Twit's Room."

CHAMPION OF THE WORLD

Vivid dioramas feature life-sized wax figures of Trump as he triumphs over world leaders. Of note: the statues of Trump are far superior to the one found in Madame Tussauds, which uses hair from red squirrels to authentically recreate his iconic look[6] ("The level of quality is not even there"—Don). Don believes the Tussauds version of him is too short, fat, mean-looking, and ugly. In the Tussauds version, Don is a 97-pound weakling, carrying 200 (ish) pounds of fat. In his library, Don's head will be set atop Rocky Balboa's body.

The exhibit brings to life many of the victorious scenes that made history (at least in Don's mind):

- See Kim Jong-un cowering as he agrees to unilateral disarmament.

- Cheer as Big Bad Vlad cowers as he agrees to not invade Western Europe.
- Laugh at recreations of your favorite "shove it" moments! Watch as Don adroitly pushes Montenegro Prime Minister Dusko Markovic out of the way to win the prime spot in front of the TV cameras! Crow along as Don uses his superior (and inflated) height to tower over "Tiny Xi" Jinping to extract massive trade concessions like the universally lauded one-cent tariff on imported bottles of soy sauce.

REPLICA ESCALATOR

A golden escalator ride changed America forever when Donald J. Trump made his grand entrance to announce his bid for the presidency on June 16, 2015 in Trump Tower, New York.

A full-scale working replica has been crafted with painstaking detail and is located near the staircase to the museum's lower level. Be sure to purchase your ticket as soon as you arrive, as capacity is limited on this popular ride. Who else but Donald J. Trump gives you a chance to feel like the ultimate winner for just $7.25 – the tower's real address on 5th Avenue? As you descend, wave and gloat at the poor losers hoofing it down the stairs. MAGA security guards will wave their pistols at visitors and hold signs that say "clap" so the applause will be deafening.

HATERS AND ROGUES GALLERY

A dungeon, Florida style, features many of the characters on Trump's revenge list, allowing visitors to experience the exhilaration of settling old scores. The centerpiece exhibit promises to enflame the emotions of red-blooded Americans. Here, a life-sized replica of Hillary Clinton is locked behind bars, offering 360-degree views into her cell so everyone gets a good look. A soundtrack mixes her "basket of deplorables" line with chants of "lock her up" and plays over and over and over, with visitors joining in the refrain.

Other highlights include a faceless mannequin with a "whistleblower" sign hanging from its neck. For an additional fee, museumgoers can vent their frustrations by tossing balls at the figure. If anyone successfully knocks off its head, the whistleblower's name and contact information are revealed! There's fun for everyone in the family here. Buy tickets so each of your little ones can throw a custard pie at the animated Adam "Shifty" Schiff, while teens can blow their allowances firing real ammo at the "Nervous Nancy" firing range.

FACTS AND EVIDENCE EXHIBIT

For his supporters, the president's word was good enough. But for the haters and doubters out there, this archive clears Trump of any wrongdoing, ever. Highlights include:

- Scientific proof that his inauguration crowd size was the best ever, PERIOD!
- Detailed evidence that Mueller's golf club membership was the reason he pursued the Russian "hoax."
- A reenactment of the "perfect" phone call where Don assured the Ukrainian president that his approval of $390 million in aid was categorically *not* conditional upon investigation of the Bidens.

THE RUSSIAN WING

Sponsored by the United Russia party, V. Putin, and "friends," this impressive wing greets museumgoers with a warm personal welcome from none other than the Russian president himself. His inspiring message envisions a future where tensions between the two counties thaw faster than the tundra. Together, Russia and America will commit to fight against climate science and, hand-in-hand, will invest in the mining and extractive industries to further exploit the earth's natural resources, create jobs, and invigorate global economies. Don is absolutely looking out for our interests here.

Also on display is Trump's bold, gold Sharpie signature across the bottom of the New Start Arms Treaty, authorizing America to buy missile systems from Moscow to protect the U.S. from Mexican attacks.

Plans for the forthcoming Trump Tower Moscow ("It will be TREMENDOUS! YUGE!") are prominently displayed in several places throughout the wing. To take advantage of the large discount offered exclusively to current museum visitors, please contact a nearby representative who will collect your deposit.

THE WALL

So many thousands of miles were planned, so few were built (and a portion collapsed in a 40-mph wind gust). Just like the Berlin Wall is exhibited at museums around the world, where pieces of the once-proud and defaced barrier serve as a symbol of what was, the wall erected at the Trump museum showcases his singular vision of what *could have been* – if only America had listened to him.

It'll be painted metallic gold (Don does love his gold) to shine and reflect the light at his museum, and as proof of the wall's superior construction, a section of it is designated for climbing by adventurous visitors (please see attendant to pay fee of $25 and sign Climbing Wall Release/Indemnification of all Claims and Covenants).

THE BIGGEST TANNING SALON IN THE ENTIRE WORLD!!!*

Predicted to be a fan favorite and big moneymaker (BIG!), this is a walk-right-in tanning salon – no reservations required. Don always had an instant tan and now you can too! For a mere $100, visitors can spend an hour on a UV sunbed, or if short on time, pick up a tube of Don's favorite cadmium Orang-U-Tan Cream for just $20. On the way out, be sure to pose for a selfie with the cardboard cut-out of the man with the orange glow.

THE OVAL OFFICE

As is customary, the museum will display a replica Oval Office. Don isn't much for hand-me-downs (he called The White House "a dump"), so he didn't do anything innovative to the design of the Oval while in office – he just switched out a few paintings and rugs and added

---

*It may not actually be the biggest in the world but hey, who cares? Minor detail in Trump's world.

gold drapes from the Clinton era (and you-know-who's favorite color). It includes photos of Trump's parents, but none of his wives or children, since he didn't display them during his term in office. Think about that for a second – no pictures of your wife or kids in your office? Weird, right? If you're a narcissist, no it isn't.

SATURATED FAT-CATS CAFE

The president is living proof that healthy eating is nothing more than liberal hysteria dreamed up by "experts" (until his arteries clog and kill him). In line with his own dietary preferences as well as a museum-wide ban on political correctness, the cafeteria scoffs at recommended daily allowances and takes advantage of relaxed food-safety regulations.

Visitors will eat like a king, just like Trump himself does, in this upscale casual eatery bedecked with gold-colored plates, cutlery, linens, and even golden trash cans.

The menu will be simple, but the portions enormous:

- The Trump Hamberder: fat and unhealthy with thick yellow cheese
- Fried Chicken: served by the bucketload; all reddish orange (clown orange to you and me)
- Trump Steak: order it cooked however you

want, but they're all served overcooked – the way Don likes them, like rocks on a plate: overdone, shriveled, and charred to the bone.

- "I love Hispanics!" Taco Bowl
- Fish Surprise: no fish, just a square of deep-fried sawdust flavored with MSG
- Coke, Diet Coke, Trump Natural Spring Water, Bottled Trump Water (i.e. tap water)
- Ice Cream: one scoop

There will be hand sanitizer dispensers at every table, at the front door to the café, and in every room of the museum. Dirty Don believes his hands can never be too clean.

PUBLIC RESTROOMS

It will be good to see Democrats and Republicans standing side by side united by a common cause (even though they'll be pissing). Designed to accommodate Don's phobia of germs, visitors can get in and out without touching the golden door handles or toilet seats, and each toilet has an automatic flush to take care of business. Visitors are reminded to wash their hands before leaving, with gold towelettes from goldfish-themed towel dispensers providing the utmost in luxury and convenience.

THE CHAPEL

The modesty of Christianity and Trump's grandiosity are clearly in conflict here. The chapel's massive and ornate gold altar is flanked by portraits of Don, the self-proclaimed "Chosen One,"[7] while very few pews are provided for the faithful. Visitors are encouraged to file in, silently gaze upon his portraits, pause at the altar, and pause again at a donation box on their way out.

Under the altar is the sacred "holy of holies" or "vault of truth" which only High Priest Don can visit. It's empty. And flooded by the rising groundwater from climate change.

THE BURIAL SITE

Even though Don is superstitious and one of the oldest presidents, the plans for his library do not spec out a grave or a memorial site. If he follows the examples of other presidential libraries, his body (or ashes) might eventually be interred on site. Presidential graves tend to be modest – often little more than an engraved metal plate on a piece of suitable stone, organically placed within the landscape, and not at all showy. Though Don is a Christian, how he strikes a balance between modesty and mania remains unknown until this design is seen. Quite likely the monument will be big and the modesty small.

REAL ESTATE OPPORTUNITIES

Trump University will be exhumed and ready to teach you the secrets of not just real estate but political success! All his tricks will be revealed in this year-long course, with tuition competitively priced at $50,000 (no refunds, no credits) ... sign-up now!

HIGH STAKES POKER LOUNGE AND SLOT MACHINES

Don has a disastrous history with casinos, losing tons of other people's money yet somehow generating a billion in tax credits for himself – so it's no surprise that the plans for his library indicate he may build out several gaming rooms. These rooms are not located on the portion of the library property that will be deeded to the U.S., allowing Dodgy Don to duck around the prohibitions preventing the federal government from running a gambling operation. Instead, he'll develop the casino on adjacent land belonging to the local Peetape Tribe (rhymes with Starbucks Frappé). Look out for the "Ukrainian Democracy Destruction" shooter games and the "Penny Falls" slots which never seem to pay out a penny.

THE MEGA-MAGA(!!!) GIFT SHOP

If you have any money left, the (for-profit) gift shop will try and part you from it. MAGA-everything is sold here: MAGA cookies, MAGA flags and hats, MAGA jams (and how to get out of them), MAGA sanitizing hand cream, MAGA spermicide, MAGAVIAGRA (get your polls up), MAGAGOOP (like WD-40 but doesn't work), MAGA pesticide (for use on Democrats), MAGA this, MAGA that, MAGA! MAGA!! MAGA!!! You'll leave exhausted and much poorer.

TRAVELING EXHIBITION

Some of the permanent artifacts, mementos, and fabrications will be on-loan to a small traveling exhibition that will circulate between the sites of various future Trump building projects including Moscow, Pyongyang, and the Trump hotel on The Moon.

WHAT WON'T BE IN IT

Books, for one. At least not many. Trump knows little about actual libraries and doesn't really read. He writes tweets but isn't capable of constructing real sentences. He simply isn't a fan of the written word. You might find a few remaindered copies of *The Art Of The Deal*. That's about it.

Plus, every piece of inbound correspondence from his tenure as president will be redacted for 100 years or so, with all the crucial elements hidden behind big black blocks.

Another other glaring omission? There's no mention of Obama anywhere in the library. No pictures of the hand-over or together at state events. Trump seems to have a deep insecurity about President Obama. Quite possibly, he feels a niggling sense of what others would recognize as shame – that Trump is a black-hearted lothario while his predecessor was a family man guided by whiter-than-white values.

Objectivity and facts are also in scant supply, despite an exhibit touting otherwise. Though all presidential libraries tend to present history in ways that paint their president in the best light, the Trump library takes on the task of polishing his legacy to a blinding extreme. Bold-faced lies were a signature of his presidency, and here in his library, they are piled up in every corner and draped over every exhibit.

His will be a museum in name only; vaudeville would be a better description. It is an all-out appeal to his base, and it will rally their basest instincts through rituals and chants.

And Trumpers will lap it up. L a p ... i t ... u p. For the reds (the Republicans, that is, not communists), a visit to his museum will be a like a stroll down memory lane, to a picture-perfect past where someone has edited out all the mistakes, errors, and inconvenient truths, *1984*-style. It will return them to the glory years, to a safer and more certain time, back to the good old days when Don was president and Big Bad Vlad wasn't actually so bad as long as the economy and stock market stayed strong.

OVERALL RATING: TWO THUMBS DOWN!!!

Chapter 4
The Truth About
Presidential Libraries —
Not Alternative Facts

I TIP MY HAT TO ANTHONY CLARK'S EXCELLENT BOOK about presidential legacies and libraries, *The Last Campaign: How Presidents Rewrite History, Run for Posterity & Enshrine Their Legacies.*[1] Much of the material here was sourced from it. It's a great follow-on read that investigates how "Unrestrained commemoration, unregulated – and undisclosed – contributions, and unchecked partisan politics have radically altered the look and purpose of presidential libraries."

If an overview of presidential libraries seems boring, jump to Chapter 5 to read about how Don will work the system and turn his library into the cash-grab to end all cash-grabs. TREMENDOUS upside potential!

There's a process behind presidential libraries. And a lot of history. I'll begin with a brief timeline and the legislation governing them.

Franklin D. Roosevelt established the first official presidential library when he donated his personal and presidential papers to the federal government in 1939.

Previously, these historical documents remained the property of the presidents, who could do with them what they wanted. They might be left to or distributed among heirs, lost or exposed to the elements, tossed in the trash, or eaten by moths.

The Presidential Libraries Act of 1955 was enacted to preserve presidential records and make the archive accessible. It laid out a system allowing for privately funded libraries to be erected, then deeded to the federal government which maintains and operates them on behalf of the American people. No federal money can be used to finance construction, though state and local governments can chip in, and no presidential library can be built on federal land (Nixon tried hard to thwart that law in California but failed). In 1986, President Reagan amended the Act, seeking to *limit* the size of the presidential libraries, in part to shift the rising cost of operations from taxpayers to private endowments.

During the same time period, other legislation was enacted that would significantly affect presidential libraries. In 1966, President Johnson signed the Freedom of Information Act (FOIA) – that bane of shady government – stipulating that the public has the right to request government documents, with access being subject to certain restrictions regarding sensitivity and secrecy.

In 1974, Congress passed the Presidential Recordings and Materials Preservation Act to specifically prevent President Nixon from burning his tapes. Finally, in 1978, the Presidential Records Act was passed, making presidential records the property of the American people, not the presidents themselves. On behalf of all Americans, the Office of Presidential Libraries administers the network of facilities and is part of the larger National Archives and Records Administration (NARA), an independent federal government agency that serves as the nation's official keeper of records.

This solemn office is entrusted with preserving the history of America and the stories of its people. NARA's vast holdings[2] currently include:

- 10 billion pages of textual records
- 12 million maps, charts, and architectural and engineering drawings
- 25 million still photographs and graphics
- 24 million aerial photographs
- 300,000 reels of motion picture film
- 400,000 video and sound recordings
- 133 terabytes of electronic data

NARA is also responsible for exhibiting the documents that originally made America great: the Declaration of Independence, the Constitution, and the Bill of Rights.

Now *that's* a solemn duty indeed. But there is and

has always been controversy about presidential records and libraries. Should all the presidents' archives be stored together in one national mega-library or should each president get to curate their own legacy, rewriting history with a little fantasy?

Chapter 5
Library or Lie-Brary?

THE WORD LIBRARY CAN CONJURE UP IMAGES OF books, of musty old papers, or learning, or of truth. Presidential libraries are a different kind of library. Most of their historical documents are preserved in repositories for use by scholars and historians.

On the other hand, members of the general public nearly always visit a president's *museum* rather than the library itself next door, getting more of an entertainment experience that portrays the president in the most flattering light. On a scale from brutally honest to "a pack of lies," Don's library will be the latter. In fact, the "truths" it portrays will fall somewhere between sycophantic slobbering and psychopathic. Lies will be whispered, shouted, shown, and sold from every room.

At each presidential museum, exhibits and programming are created, curated, and funded by a private foundation, which presents the president's legacy in any way it sees fit, without government oversight.

Who might fund exhibitions at Trump's museum? Well, let's see: the Russian Federation (thank you Vlad), the NRA, Sheldon Adelson, the Koch brothers, Evangelicals ("he's such a good man!"), and various odd billionaires who want to curry favor with him and his family.

Who might Don tap to head his library's independent foundation? Knowing his penchant for nepotism, he won't look far, not with stupendous progeny like Donald Jr., Eric, and Ivanka with Jared to choose from. There's no one more qualified to spin this infamous fabulist's legacy.

Other presidential libraries charge admission fees and sell mementos. Trump's library and museum will be a gluttonous profit-center for banqueting and conferences with a gift shop the size of a big-box retail store, a tanning salon, and a yuuuge television studio for his new Fox TV show. If located at Mar-a-Lago, his spectacular residence will be attached to his library; if at Doral, it'll include the presidential golf club, only now with mind-boggling green fees and "extensive retail offerings spread throughout the property."[1]

The library part will be run by an archivist appointed by Trump. This person will be more of a propagandist who in the least, protects Don's image and at most, pushes for his canonization. This role seems like a typical "crony" appointment, so Brad Parscale, who headed the successful digital media efforts of the 2016 and the failed efforts of the 2020 campaign, immediately comes to mind. He's uniquely un-objective and biased – a perfect fit in the world according to Trump.

But the job does involve real work and skills, so the appointee ought to have *some* relevant experience ... so no to Parscale, no to Alex Jones, and no to "Spicey" Sean.

The libraries are not meant to be political operations, but there are many ways to skirt the rules – so they often do. Don likes skirts and hates rules, so you know skirts will be lifted and rules bent or broken.

Any section of Trump's library that *costs* money to run will be part of the facility's federal operations. Any part that *makes* money will remain under private ownership so Trump can exploit its profits. Site plans showing which areas are federal and which are private will look like a Rorschach inkblot, a patchwork as crazy as North Carolina's 12th electoral district – the most gerrymandered in the nation.

Trump's replica Oval Office can be yours for the day, for the right price. Next to the museum there will be several replica Lincoln Bedrooms rentable by the night. Throughout the whole museum, the Feds will clean the bathrooms at the government's expense (just as the nation had to clean up all the sh*t Trump left behind) and Don will pocket the money from all the concessions. As he said regarding his tax returns, "That makes me smart, right?[2]

You think I joke?

His library will straddle private gain and public duty just as effortlessly as Trump has during his entire time in office. He smirks, he denies it, and he shrugs – but he knows what he's doing all along.

Following Trump's presidency, there will be researchers who want to access his records in search for the truth, and others who want to use it to propagandize or canonize him.

For five years after he leaves office, his presidential records will be available only to Congress, the courts, Don, and his successor. For up to 20 years – long after he has passed on – "classified" privileges could be asserted to deny FOIA requests for his presidential records, especially those which could further taint his tainted legacy. Many fights will remain over access to his legal matters, and Don does love a legal fight. My guess is that his presidential library will help many, many lawyers make a lot of money, long after he's gone up to heaven.

Regarding his legacy, I don't think it's that important to Don. On the occasions that the rattling pea in his mind settles in the right spot, he may realize his age. But he's a man who lives in the moment, not thinking much about the past or planning for the future. Now is it.

But Trump's always been driven by ratings and popularity and crowd size, so if he gave a thought to his future library, it would be to attendance. We don't need accountants with worksheets or advanced algorithms to forecast attendance at Don's library. Unless he is disgraced and sentenced, it will probably be record-breaking.

Both the unwashed and godly will converge on Mar-a-Lago which is no longer just a building, but the WWE or Super Bowl of libraries. Over time, it will become a shrine. It won't be modest, it won't be very serious, and it won't be truthful, but it will tremendous fun or extremely handwringing, depending your political color. It will be the most Trumpian place on earth. It may also be the *last* Trumpian place on earth because every other once-Trump building will have either removed his name from its branding or gone broke.

Chapter 6
The Biggest Loser!
The "Stolen" Election of
2020!

ON WEDNESDAY, NOVEMBER 4, 2020, DONALD Trump will wake up a loser. The biggest loser ever! Period! Don's sanity and world peace will hang in the balance. His first thought will be, "What Would Jesus Do?" No, it won't! Of course, it won't!! His first thought will be, "I was robbed!"

In the 11 dangerous weeks remaining in his presidency, the winner will become a whiner. He'll go see foreign leaders to talk up Trump Moscow and Trump Pyongyang, but their demeanors will have changed. Noses will wrinkle from their new "shit on my shoe" attitude toward the stupid orange clown, this soon-to-be-a-footnote in history, while they keep a firm but white-knuckled grip on their power.

> "If I don't win you're going to see a crash like you've never seen before."[1]

Don will go into full denial/victim mode: He will pronounce a new stock market crash to try to make the markets go to new lows. He will pardon his donors and anyone who ever helped him and didn't rat him out. He will claim electoral fraud and launch multiple investigations to prove that over 10 million votes were cast by Mexicans, Ukrainians, dead criminals and members of the press who were out to get him. He will likely implode like a dark star – but the silence will be deafening because all of us will have quickly turned the page and moved forward and on to the next president, with hope in our hearts and the promise of a little warmth in the January sunshine.

Genetically, Don cannot accept losing. So, he'll re-diagnose this as the election that was stolen! That's it! – a conspiracy and a grudge that Don can run with for years. He does so love a grudge and conspiracy: it fuels his negative energy, rage, and bile; it angers and energizes him, and will give him endless material for his TV show co-hosted with Alex Jones.

All the events and his pronouncements between this day and when he vacates the office on January 20, 2021 will be glossed over by his museum. An exhibit will explain the greatest conspiracy in the history of the universe. The FBI worked in secret with the media, liberal elites, COVID-19 virus labs, Barack Obama, a shoal of alien great white sharks, rigged voting machines, and the Knights Templar. They used a whole smorgasbord of illegal tactics like lies, fake news, wiretapping, and the covfefe virus to suppress Republican voters. On the big day, unexplained magnetic energy was beamed from space, deterring Rust Belt voters from coming out to vote. Even the Russian media pronounced it a gigantic **заговор** ("conspiracy"), and that's not FAKE NEWS. Sad! So sad!

JANUARY 20, 2021

The transition of power to the incoming Democratic president will be chaotic and incomplete even if Don wants to help. But he won't. He won't be generous; he'll be grievous and grudging. It will be very hard for Don to dodge a meeting at the White House or shaking the new president's hand (coronavirus will be his excuse), but he'll try. Think about the skin-to-skin contact of that handshake. It'll be like grabbing broken glass for Don, to look into the eyes of the man who crushed him, those eyes proud and smiling.

But he *will* dodge the swearing-in. Trump will want to give the new president the middle finger for whooping him, and that poker face of his will pucker petulantly in a dead giveaway. Instead, he'll play golf that day, scoring a 91 but recording it as a 74. That's just the way he and his golf balls roll.

The inaugural celebrations will be intense, the joy manifest, and the Republican party silent ... but not Don. He'll be tweeting up a storm of nutty falsehoods and lies from his Florida sunbed (best-looking former president ever!).

Do we like bad losers? Do we like a losing quarterback who punctures the football, or a family member who tips over the Monopoly board when they land on their sister's hotel? Even as a sore and bitter loser, Don will still have the power to make Americans angry and depressed.

And as his last act as president, he'll tuck the keys to 1600 Pennsylvania Avenue under the doormat with a nice note that says, "Fuck you!"

JANUARY 21, 2021 — FANTASY EDITION

He's history! Melania serves him with divorce papers. The Russians leak documents showing they loaned Agent Orange ten billion dollars – he really *is* a foreign agent and going to jail!

JANUARY 21, 2021 — ACTUALLY

Don will be on to the next thing – or really, back to the old thing, which is using a TV show to pretend he's making billions of dollars while somehow bringing in just enough cash to shuffle his debts and debtors long enough to stay afloat. He'll be based at Mar-a-Lago where he will build and use a TV studio next to his museum for the adulation and the worship and the money TV will generate.

And if his health holds up and the polls look good –

who knows? – he might well run for governor of Florida in 2026. Maybe you Floridians aren't quite off the hook yet!

THE TRUMP ORANGE SHOW

Get ready for a Fox Primetime line-up change. We might see a co-piloted Hannity Presidential Show, or maybe Trump will go solo. Don't worry Republicans, that sweet cadmium orange glow will still shine into your living room every weekday evening. He'll predict every coming disaster after-the-fact. He'll compare every policy error or unlucky break in the present to his perfect presidency in the past, and soon he'll have recast the Trump years as a gentle breath of fresh air instead of the seething storm of moral turpitude that *we* remember. The stock market was perfect back in 2020 (wait – didn't it fall?). Were we not the envy of the world? (No, we were not!) He hired the most talented team ever (and fired them all over and over again). You know the drill because Dentist Don has been taking it to our molars for the past four years. Seeing history through his eyes will require a squint so narrow you'll be walking round blind.

Trump can sell diet pills and he-man supplements Alex Jones-style.[2] He can peddle his university again (or maybe a "You Can Be President Too!" course). Like a bloated walrus sunning itself, Don can bask in the applause and adulation all day long.

REVISIONISM

It was Churchill who said, "History is written by the victors." Over the 2021–2025 term, Congress will likely get, and the national media will publish, Don's personal tax returns which will puncture the money myth. The Russians will withdraw his personal credit. Lawsuits will swirl around his alleged infidelities and grift. Multiple congressional committees will start new "witch hunts," flying around on broomsticks and subpoenaing documents by the thousand. Trump had better lawyer up while he can still afford to. Bloomberg will buy Trump's golf courses out of Chapter 11.

This whole process will take years, and Don may or may not survive it. He's lived his whole life as a media stooge – it's second nature to him – and now he'll have a personal and perpetual ax to grind for the rest of his life and grind it he will. Every time there's an economic slump, or a plane crash, or a yeti is spotted in the wilds of Alaska, we'll hear him trot out the same old sh*t again: the election was "stolen" by the "fake news media," his presidency was the best ever, and by the way, Barack Obama was not born in the United States.

Meanwhile, will his museum stick to its original "hero" script? Or will there be a revision demoting

Trump to "flawed hero"? Or perhaps, under political pressure, NARA will downsize his museum's budget, sending Don from hero to zero.

Trump will be as controversial in the rear-view mirror as he was through the windshield. He will be the best president ever and the worst president ever. Getting and commanding attention was always his primary ambition and even his detractors must admit he has an unparalleled ability to do that ... not that that's a good thing.

FACTS AND FICTION

The Trump Presidential Library and Museum will probably be the most visited, the most liked, and the most tweeted about in history. It will be packed full of lies yet filled with the sighs of the faithful. And Trump will milk them for the money. They'll be conned into becoming a member, mega-member, MAGA-member, or whatever they call their pyramid-scheme of promises offering the promise of a fist-bump with big Don to a lucky few.

Maps in his library will be redrawn with a Sharpie. Numbers will be inflated. Gross acts literally crossed out of history. And his supporters will still lap it up, because its taste is warm and sweet and familiar. Democrats will spit that swill to the ground and demand the truth be told no matter how salty or sour it is ... yet they will come to his museum. They will come.

For all its marble and gold, animatronics, witch hunts, lies, and exaggerations, his museum *will* bring us all together but back to a time when we were very, very divided.

Good night and good luck, Don!

P.S. GULP ... WHAT IF HE ACTUALLY WINS IN 2020?

Afterword
Vote Vote Vote!

DON WILL GET HIS PRESIDENTIAL MUSEUM IN WEST Palm Beach, Florida circa 2026. I'll be visiting it (incognito) no matter whether he's still at liberty or incarcerated or incapacitated or dead. Maybe you will too. Regardless, you can help make Don's library a reality sooner rather than later by ticking the box for Joe Biden in November.

Now it's time for me to go and soon, it'll be time for Don to head off to the sun and let the country's wounds start to heal. It's time for civility, for political ceasefire, and perhaps even time to start seeing the merit in some of the other party's ideas and beliefs. Personally, I hope the word compromise can be washed, spun, and dried so it is no longer a dirty word. I hope the saner Trumpublicans revert back into being Republicans. I hope true dialogue is encouraged, reforms make electoral districts fairer, and Citizen's United is repealed which will help drain the swamp of political donations.

And pigs might fly.

And when you fly into South Florida, into the gold-colored DJT/Donald Trump International Airport, and take those gold-colored, coal-fired Trump buses to his museum, I hope you'll remember this book. While Donald John Trump didn't make America great again, he *did* clearly show us how divisive and angry we could be, how badly-off we are when we have a bad leader, and how much better his successor can be at unifying the country, taking us forward together, and inspiring *all* Americans to do better and be better.

Vote! Vote! Vote! Vote as many times as you legally able!*

---

*One or zero times.

Appendix
Additional Resources

Alioto, Daisy. "From Nixon to Obama-What Presidential Libraries Say about the Leaders Who Built Them." *Artsy*, 7 July 2017. www.artsy.net/article/artsy-editorial-nixon-obama-presidential-libraries-leaders-built.

Anderson, David. "A Visit to the Trump Presidential Library and Casino in 2017." *Democracy Chronicles*, 18 May 2017. democracychronicles.org/trump-presidential-library.

"At A Presidential Library, Lessons From Truman For Trump." *WAMC*, 25 Oct. 2017. wamc.org/post/presidential-library-lessons-truman-trump.

Beliveau, Severin M. "Presidential Libraries Are a Waste of Money." *Press Herald*, 17 June 2017. pressherald.com/2017/06/18/maine-voices-presidential-libraries-are-a-waste-of-money.

Brashich, Deyan R. "Opening of the Donald J Trump Presidential Library." *Contrary Views*, 5 May 2018. deyan-brashich.com/home/2018/5/5/opening-of-the-donald-j-trump-presidential-library.html.

Burbank, Whitney. "Commissioners Ponder Proposal for Trump Presidential Library in Palm Beach County." *WPBF*, WPBF, 7 Oct. 2017. wpbf.com/article/commissioners-ponder-proposal-for-trump-presidential-library-in-palm-beach-county/8693518#.

Carr, Taylor. "The Donald J. Trump Presidential Library, Hotel & Casino." *Bullshit.ist,* 5 Nov. 2016. bull-shit.ist/the-donald-j-trump-presidential-library-hotel-casino-4c3bd0cfc3f8.

Clark, Anthony. "Presidential Libraries Are Huge Failures." *Salon*, Salon.com, 25 Apr. 2013. salon.com/2013/04/25/presidential_libraries_are_huge_failures.

Clark, Anthony. *The Last Campaign: How Presidents Rewrite History, Run for Posterity & Enshrine Their Legacies*. Anthony Clark, 2015.

Clark, Anthony. "Presidential Libraries Are a Scam. Could Obama Change That?" *POLITICO Magazine*, 7 May 2017. politico.com/magazine/story/2017/05/07/presidential-libraries-are-a-scam-could-obama-change-that-215109.

Connelly, Matthew. "Why You May Never Learn the Truth About ICE." *The New York Times,* 4 Feb. 2020. nytimes.com/2020/02/04/opinion/archives-document-destruction.html.

Crockett Jr., Stephen A. "Trump Has the Perfect Location for His Library: A Trump-Owned Property." *The Root*, 24 June 2019. theroot.com/trump-has-the-perfect-location-for-his-library-a-trump-1835804564.

Crosbie, Jack. "Obama's Presidential Library Is Kind Of a Bummer." *Splinter News*, 21 Feb. 2019. splinternews.-com/obamas-presidential-library-could-set-a-bad-precedent-f-1832792663.

Cross, David P. *Chasing History: One Man's Roadtrip Through the Presidential Libraries*. Stone and Patrick Publishers, 2014.

Cross, David P. "Presidential Library Sites Offer New Ways to Understand the Leaders." *Washington Post*, 13 Jan. 2015. washingtonpost.com/opinions/presidential-library-sites-offer-new-ways-to-understand-the-leaders/2015/01/13/e3ad4af8-9b27-11e4-bcfb-059ec7a93ddc_story.html.

Dodge, Arnold. "Lines Will Be Forming Soon for the Trump Presidential Library." *Long Island News from the Long Island Press*, 25 May 2016. longislandpress.com/2016/05/28/lines-will-be-forming-soon-for-the-trump-presidential-library.

"Donald Trump Library." Image. *Imgur*, 22 May 2018. imgur.com/gallery/IdcAS.

"Donald J. Trump Presidential Library." Image. *Eduhacker*, 10 May 2017. eduhacker.net/libraries/donald-j-trump-presidential-library.html.

Fahrenthold, David. Twitter Post. 8 Nov. 2019, 8:30 PM. twitter.com/Fahrenthold/status/1192615325470203904.

Fausset, Richard, et al. "Impeachment Then and Now: What Three Presidential Sites Can Teach Us." *The New York Times*, The New York Times, 1 Feb. 2020. nytimes.com/2020/02/01/us/impeachment-lessons-trump.html.

Forsberg-Wilson O'Donnell, Becky. "The Bully Pulpit on Display: How Presidential Libraries Present Presidential History." *Research Works*, 2018. digital.lib.washington.edu/researchworks/handle/1773/42021.

Frank, Jeffrey. "A Future Visit to the Donald J. Trump Presidential Library." *The New Yorker*, The New Yorker,

19 June 2017. newyorker.com/news/daily-comment/a-future-visit-to-the-donald-j-trump-presidential-library.

Frum, David. Twitter Post. 10 Oct. 2019, 9:24 PM. twitter.com/davidfrum/status/ 1182467047965548544?lang=en.

Henning Santiago, Amanda Luz. "Putting Trump's Presidential Library on Staten Island Is a Great Idea." *CSNY*, 30 Sept. 2019. cityandstateny.com/articles/politics/new-york-city/putting-trumps-presidential-library-on-staten-island-is-actually-great.

Hufbauer, Benjamin. *Presidential Temples: How Memorials and Libraries Shape Public Memory*. Univ. Press of Kansas, 2006.

Jacobson, Scott, et al. "Exclusive First Look: The Donald J. Trump Presidential Library and Museum." *Vanity Fair*, Vanity Fair, 10 Nov. 2015. vanityfair.com/culture/2015/11/donald-trump-presidential-library-and-museum.

Johnson, Steve. "A Look Forward at the Trump Presidential Library." *The Chicago Tribune*, 22 May 2019. chicagotribune.com/entertainment/ct-a-look-forward-at-the-trump-presidential-library-20161122-column.html.

Kanter, Jodi. *Presidential Libraries As Performance: Curating American Character From Herbert Hoover to George W. Bush*. Southern Illinois University Press, 2016.

Kushner, Malcolm. "The Trump Presidential Library." *HuffPost*, HuffPost, 30 Dec. 2016. huffpost.-com/entry/the-trump-presidential-li_b_8891614.

Lantzer, Jason S. "The Public History of Presidential Libraries: How the Presidency Is Presented to the People." *Journal of the Association for History and Computing*, vol. 6, no. 1, Apr. 2003. quod.lib.umich.e-du/j/jahc/3310410.0006.101/--public-history-of-presiden-tial-libraries-how-the-presidency.

Levinson, Martin. "Welcome to the Donald J. Trump Presidential Library." *The Satirist*, 5 Oct. 2019. hesatirist.com/satires/welcome-to-the-donald-j-trump-presidential-library.html.

Lowell Sun Editorial Staff. "Words of Wisdom for Trump's Presidential Library." *Lowell Sun*, 11 July 2019. lowellsun.com/2018/05/20/words-of-wisdom-for-trumps-presidential-library.

Luscombe, Richard. "'It Makes Sense': the Trailer Park That Could Be Trump's Presidential Library." *The*

Guardian, Guardian News and Media, 10 Jan. 2020. theguardian.com/us-news/2020/jan/10/trump-presidential-library-florida-briny-breezes.

Lynch, Suzanne. "Presidential Libraries Are Uniquely American. Will the next Be Uniquely Trumpian?" *The Irish Times*, The Irish Times, 11 Nov. 2017. irishtimes.com/news/world/us/presidential-libraries-are-uniquely-american-will-the-next-be-uniquely-trumpian-1.3287474.

Lyons, Carolyn. "All the Presidents' Libraries." *The Guardian*, 26 Oct. 2010. theguardian.com/travel/2010/oct/26/us-presidents-libraries-california.

Mann, Elana. "The Donald J. Trump Presidential Library, a Collaboration with Jean-Paul Leonard," Jan. 2017. elanamann.com/news/donald-j-trump-presidential-library-collaboration-jean-paul-leonard.

Milano, Roseann. Twitter Post. 7 Nov. 2019, 11:02 PM. twitter.com/RoseannMilano/status/1192653654181834758.

Morran, Chris. "George Conway Mocks Idea of a Trump Presidential Library as a 'Double Oxymoron.'" *Newsweek*, 23 June 2019. newsweek.com/george-conway-mocks-idea-trump-presidential-library-double-oxymoron-1445444.

Paddock, Anne. "Imagine the Donald Trump Presidential Library." *Paddock Post*, 27 Sept. 2018. paddockpost.-com/2018/09/21/imagine-the-donald-trump-presidential-library.

Reynolds, Jamie D. *Presidential Libraries: Elements and Considerations*. Nova Science Publishers, 2011.

Seeman, Joe. "Central Park Leads Site Selection for Trump Presidential Library, but Philly and DC Are Still in Running." *Buffalo Chronicle*, 1 Oct. 2019. buffalochron-icle.com/2019/09/29/central-park-leads-site-selection-for-trump-presidential-library-but-philly-and-dc-are-still-in-running.

Senik, Troy. "News of the Future: The Trump Presidential Library [Satire]." *Center for Individual Freedom*, 18 July 2015. cfif.org/v/index.php/commentary/54-state-of-affairs/2643-news-of-the-future-the-trump-presidential-library-satire.

Stahl, Michael. "Someday, Donald Trump Will Have a Presidential Library. What Will It Look like?" *QZ*, 20 Dec. 2017. qz.com/1162244/donald-j-trump-presidential-library-and-museum-what-will-it-look-like.

Stone, Paul Steven. "Welcome to the Donald J. Trump

Presidential Library." *A Stones Throw - Damn Good Blog*, 21 Jan. 2020. paulstonesthrow.com/welcome-to-the-donald-j-trump-presidential-library.

Suebsaeng, Asawin. "Don Jr. and Vanilla Ice Deny Plan for Trump Library in Palm Beach." *The Daily Beast*, The Daily Beast Company, 23 Dec. 2019. thedailybeast.-com/don-jr-and-vanilla-ice-deny-working-together-to-turn-a-palm-beach-trailer-park-into-trump-library.

The Daily Show With Trevor Noah. *Donald J. Trump Presidential Twitter Library*. Random House Publishing Group, 2018.

Trudeau, Gary. *The Far Side*, 12 Dec. 2019. gocomics.-com/doonesbury/2019/12/29.

"Trump Presidential Library Plans Announced." *Fair City News RSS*, 15 Nov. 2016. faircitynews.-com/2016/11/15/trump-presidential-library-plans-announced.

Wade, Peter. "Trump Will Look to Profit Off His Presidential Library." *Rolling Stone*, 23 June 2019. rolling-stone.com/politics/politics-news/trump-profit-presidential-library-851557.

"Why Presidential Libraries Are Controversial." *The Economist*, 25 Apr. 2019. economist.com/the-economist-explains/2019/04/25/why-presidential-libraries-are-controversial.

Acknowledgements

Thanks and Acknowledgement to

B+J+CJ+K

for your forbearance and encouragement.

ENDNOTES

INTRODUCTION: OH, YES. EVERY PRESIDENT GETS ONE!

1. Orwell, George. 1984. London: Secker and Warburg, 1949. The Internet Archive (p. 95). archive.org/details/Orwell1984prey-wo/page/n93/mode/2up/search/%22The+past+was+erased%22 (accessed March 10, 2020).

CHAPTER 1: DECISIONS, DECISIONS!

1. Trump, Donald. "Town Hall: Des Moines Iowa." *Donald Trump Holds a Town Hall-Style Event*. December 11, 2015. factba.se/transcript/donald-trump-speech-des-moines-ia-december-11-2015.

2. Freed, Benjamin. "Luxury Travel Group Gives Trump's DC Hotel a Brutal Review." *Washingtonian*, Washingtonian Media Inc., 21 Dec. 2016. washingtonian.com/2016/12/20/travel-group-dc-trump-hotel-one-worlds-worst-new-luxury-hotels.

3. Fahrenthold, David and O'Connell, Jonathan. "Trump's Prized Doral Resort Is in Steep Decline, According to Company Documents, Showing His Business Problems Are Mounting." The Washington Post. WP Company, May 15, 2019. washingtonpost.com/politics/trumps-prized-doral-resort-is-in-steep-decline-according-to-company-documents-showing-his-business-problems-are-mounting/2019/05/14/03cc701a-6b54-11e9-be3a-33217240a539_story.html.

4. Clough, Alexandra. "Trump and Related Group: The Story behind Trump Tower Palm Beach." The Palm Beach Post. The Palm Beach Post, February 21, 2017. palmbeachpost.com/busi-

ness/trump-and-related-group-the-story-behind-trump-tower-palm-beach/yNgkncIJTNmg2rlY7ktL5K/.

5. Wikipedia contributors, "List of largest houses in the United States," *Wikipedia, The Free Encyclopedia,* en.wikipedi-a.org/wiki/List_of_largest_houses_in_the_United_States (accessed March 10, 2020).

6. Trump, Donald. Twitter Post. May 13, 2015, 8:23 AM. twitter.com/realdonaldtrump/status/598463630288560128.

7. York, Peter. "Donald Trump Has a 'Dictator Chic' Design Taste." POLITICO Magazine, 2017. politico.com/magazine/sto-ry/2017/03/trump-style-dictator-autocrats-design-214877.

8. Trump, Donald. Twitter Post. July 30, 2013, 10:30 AM. twitter. com/realDonaldTrump/status/362218621428187137?ref_src= twsrc%5Etfw%7Ctwcamp%5Etweetembed%7Ctwterm% 5E362218621 428187137&ref_url=https%3A%2F%2Fdailyreckon-ing.com%2Ftop-10-donald-trump-tweets-gold%2F

9. Vilfranc, Jenifer M. "Thickness of Gold Leaf." The Physics Factbook, 1999. hypertextbook.com/facts/1999/JeniferVil-franc.shtml.

CHAPTER 2: THEM THAT CAME BEFORE HIM — 14 PRESIDENTIAL LIBRARIES

1. "How Much Have U.S. Presidents Earned Through the Years?" Salary.com, March 14, 2019. salary.com/passages/history-of-pres-idential-salaries/3/.

CHAPTER 3: THE GUIDED TOUR

1. Trump, Donald. Twitter Post. May 8, 2013, 9:37 PM. twitter.-com/realDonaldTrump/status/332308211321425920.

2. Trump, Donald. Twitter Post. January 2, 2018, 7:49 PM. twitter.-com/realDonaldTrump/status/948355557022420992.

3. Trump, Donald. Twitter Post. March 22, 2018, 6:19 AM. twitter.com/realDonaldTrump/status/976765417908776963.

4. Trump, Donald. Deleted Twitter Post. May 31, 2017, 12:06 AM. Retrieved from factba.se/search#Despite%2Bthe%2Bconstant%2Bnegative%2Bpress%2Bcovfefe.

5. Trump, Donald. Twitter Post. September 28, 2014, 8:21 PM. twitter.com/realDonaldTrump/status/516382177798680576.

6. Hassan, Jennifer, and Rick Noack. "Trump Canceled His Trip to the U.S. Embassy in London, but His Madame Tussauds Waxwork Made It." The Washington Post. WP Company, January 12, 2018. washingtonpost.com/news/world-views/wp/2018/01/12/trump-canceled-his-trip-to-the-us-embassy-in-london-but-his-waxwork-made-it/.

7. Trump, Donald. Press Gaggle before Marine One Departure. August 24, 2019. Transcript retrieved from factba.se/transcript/donald-trump-press-gaggle-marine-one-departure-august-21-2019.

CHAPTER 4: THE TRUTH ABOUT PRESIDENTIAL LIBRARIES: NOT ALTERNATIVE FACTS

1. Clark, Anthony. *The Last Campaign: How Presidents Rewrite History, Run for Posterity & Enshrine Their Legacies*. Anthony Clark, 2015.

2. "About the National Archives of the United States." General Information Leaflet, Number 1. National Archives and Records Administration. Accessed March 11, 2020. archives.gov/publications/general-info-leaflets/1-about-archives.html.

CHAPTER 5: LIBRARY OR LIE-BRARY?

1. "Golf Information." Trump National Doral Miami. trumphotels.com/miami/course-rates (accessed March 10, 2020).

2. "First Presidential Debate Between Donald Trump and Hillary Clinton." Hofstra University, Hempstead New York. September 26, 2016. Transcript retrieved from fact-ba.se/search#%22That%2Bmakes%2Bme%2Bsmart/

CHAPTER 6: THE BIGGEST LOSER! — THE "STOLEN" ELECTION OF 2020!

1. Owusu, Tony. "President Trump Predicts Market Crash If Not Re-Elected." TheStreet, February 25, 2020. thestreet.com/investing/trump-warns-market-crash-if-not-re-elected.

2. Brown, Seth. "Alex Jones's Infowars Media Empire Is Built to Sell Snake-Oil Diet Supplements." Intelligencer. New York Magazine, May 4, 2017. nymag.com/intelligencer/2017/05/how-does-alex-jones-make-money.html.